Unit 0		2
Unit 1	My School	5
Unit 2	My Toys	9
Unit 3	My Family	13
Unit 4	My Body	17
Units 1–4 Review		21
Unit 5	Stories	23
Unit 6	I Like Food	27
Unit 7	Clothes	31
Unit 8	Animals	35
Units 5–8 Review		39
Cutouts		57

WORKBOOK
STARTER

SERIES EDITORS
JoAnn (Jodi) Crandall
Joan Kang Shin

AUTHOR
Diane Pinkley

Este livro é uma versão especial. As páginas de 41 a 56 foram suprimidas para atender com exatidão às necessidades metodológicas da edição.

A paginação obedece aos padrões internacionais originais, no entanto, você poderá encontrar as páginas extraídas em www.culturainglesasp.com.br para download.

Australia • Brazil • Mexico • Singapore • United Kingdom • United States

Unit 0

1 **Listen.** Look and circle. TR: 2

1.

2.

3.

2 **Listen and circle.** TR: 3

1.    yes   no

2.    yes   no

3.    yes   no

3 Listen. Color and say. TR: 4

1.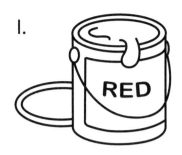
2.

4 Listen. Color and say. TR: 5

5 Look. Count and write.

6 Listen. Draw and color. TR: 6

3

7 Listen and say. TR: 7

8 Listen and look. Which word is different? Circle. TR: 8

1.

2.

9 Listen and chant. Point. TR: 9

Hello, hello.
Hi there, hi.

Time to go.
Bye, goodbye!

Unit 1
My School

1 **Listen.** Look and circle. TR: 10

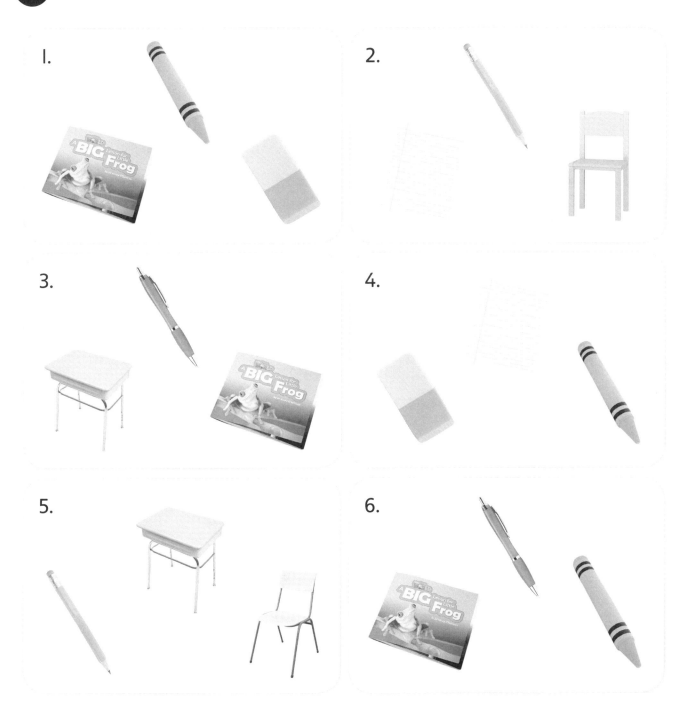

2 **Listen and say.** TR: 11

3 **Cut out the cards on page 57.** Listen. Glue the cards. Say. TR: 12

4 **Match.** Say.

5 **Listen.** Color and say. TR: 13

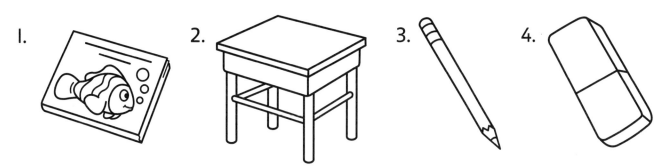

6 **Listen.** Color. Count and say. TR: 14

7 **Listen.** Count and write. TR: 15

8 Listen and say. TR: 16

9 Listen and look. Which word is different? Circle. TR: 17

1.
2.
3.

10 Listen and chant. Say a new verse. TR: 18

I have some
I have a
I have a
Let's draw again!

I have an
I have a
I have some
Let's draw again!

Unit 2
My Toys

1 **Listen.** Look and circle. TR: 19

2 **Listen and say.** TR: 20

3 **Cut out the cards on page 57.** Listen. What is it? Glue the cards. Say. TR: 21

4 **Draw your favorite toy.** Color. What is it? Say.

5 **Listen.** Color and say. TR: 22

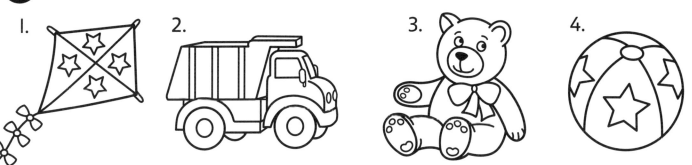

6 **Listen.** Color. Count and say. TR: 23

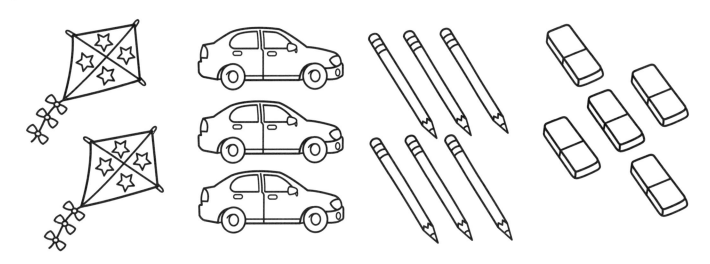

7 **Listen.** Count and write. TR: 24

8 **Listen and say.** TR: 25

9 **Listen and look.** Which word is different? Circle. TR: 26

1.

2.

3.

10 **Listen and chant.** Say a new verse. TR: 27

and ___ and more toys.
___ and ___ for girls and boys!

and ___ and more toys.
___ and ___ for girls and boys!

Unit 3
My Family

1 **Listen and look.** Draw a line. TR: 28

13

2 Listen and say. TR: 29

Who's this?

It's my sister.

3 Listen and circle. TR: 30

1.   2.   3.

4 Listen and say. TR: 31

Where's Mother?

In the living room

5 Cut out the cards on page 59. Listen. Where's the family? Glue the cards. Say. TR: 32

6 Listen. Color and say. TR: 33

1.
2.
3.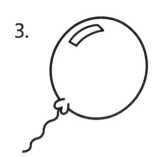
4.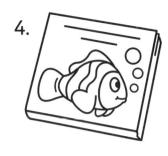

7 Listen. Color. Count and say. TR: 34

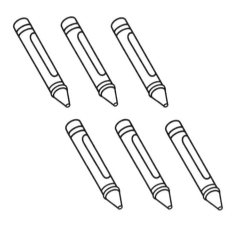
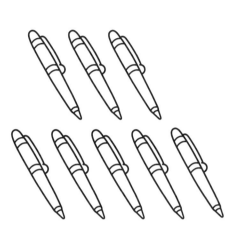
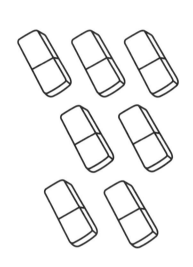

8 Listen. Count and write. TR: 35

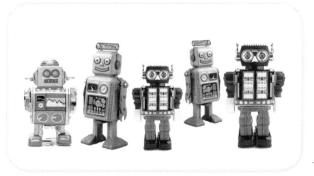

15

9 Listen and say. TR: 36

10 Listen and look. Which word is different? Circle. TR: 37

1.

2.

3.

11 Listen and chant. Say a new verse. TR: 38

I love my

Oh yes, I do.

My  and my

love him, too.

I love my

Oh yes, I do.

My and my

love her, too.

Unit 4
My Body

1 **Listen and look.** Draw a line. TR: 39

17

2 Listen and say. TR: 40

3 Listen and circle. Say. TR: 41

1.
2.
3.
4.

4 Cut out the cards on page 59. Listen and look. Glue the cards. Say. TR: 42

5 Listen. Color and say. TR: 43

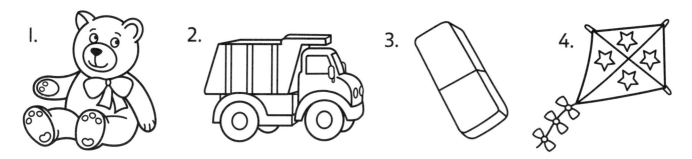

6 Listen. Color. Count and say. TR: 44

7 Listen. Count and write. TR: 45

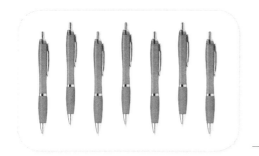

19

8 Listen and say. TR: 46

9 Listen and look. Which word is different? Circle. TR: 47

1.

2.

3.

10 Listen and chant. Say a new verse. TR: 48

One for me.   No for me.

Two  for you.   Brown for you.

Two for me.   A for me,

Two for you.   and , too.
                                          mustache

Units 1-4
Review

1 Listen. Look and circle. TR: 49

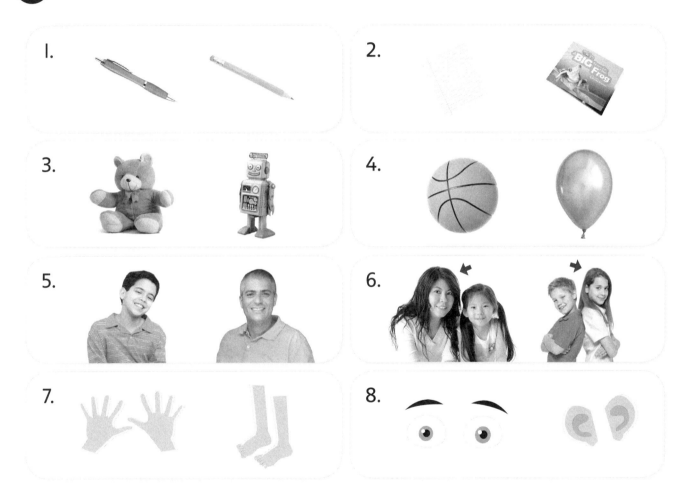

2 Listen and color. TR: 50

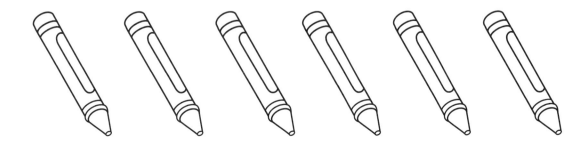

21

3 Listen. Look and circle. TR: 51

4 Listen. Count and circle. TR: 52

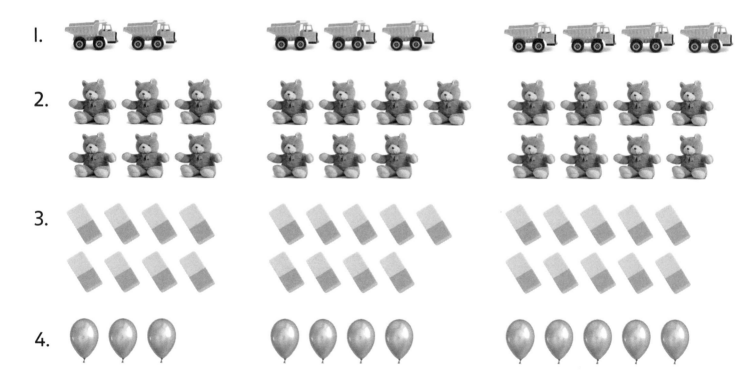

Unit 5
Stories

1 **Listen.** Look and circle. TR: 53

2 **Listen.** Draw. TR: 54

1.

2.

3 **Listen and say.** TR: 55

4 **Cut out the cards on page 61.** Listen. Glue the cards. Say. TR: 56

5 **Draw.** What do you want? Say. Color.

6 Listen. Color and say. TR: 57

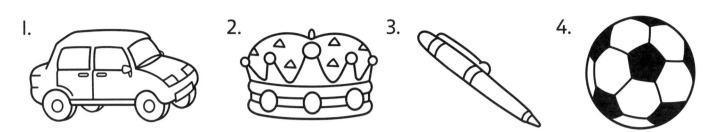

7 Listen. Color. Count and say. TR: 58

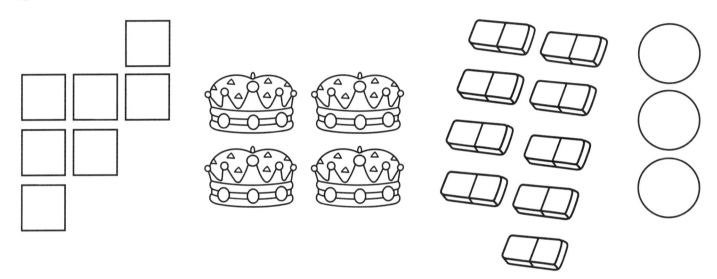

8 Listen. Count and write. TR: 59

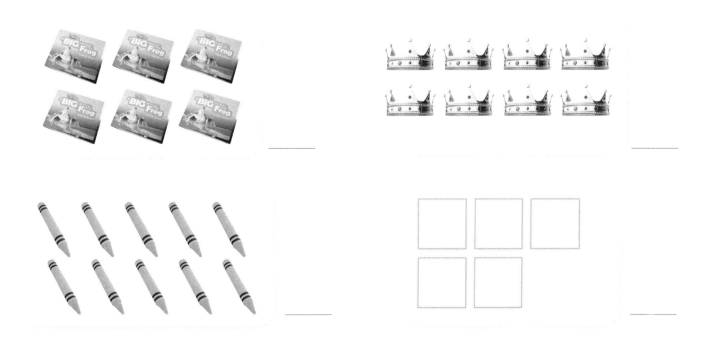

25

9 Listen and say. TR: 60

10 Listen and look. Which word is different? Circle. TR: 61

1.

2.

3.

11 Listen and chant. Say a new verse. TR: 62

The wants silver.

The wants gold.

The wants a of silver *and* gold!

The wants silver.

The wants gold.

The wants a of silver *and* gold!
ring

26

Unit 6
I Like Food

1 **Listen.** Look and circle. TR: 63

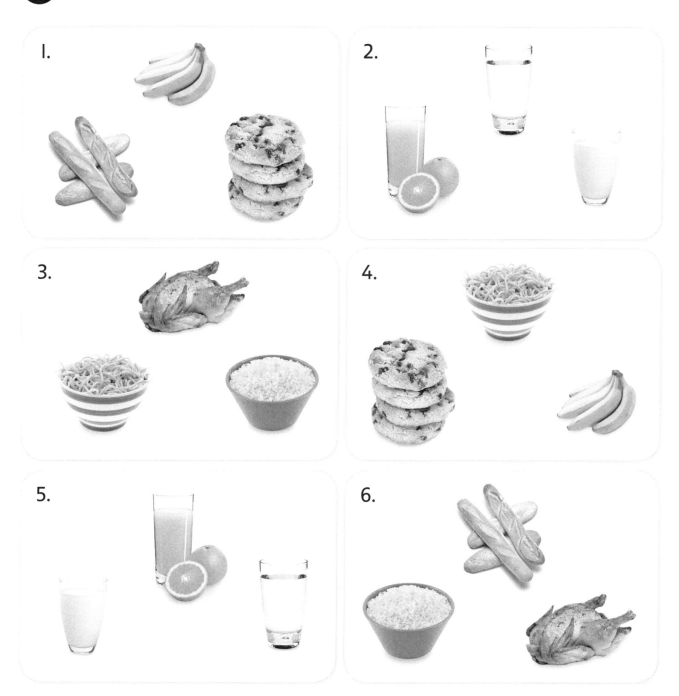

2 **Listen and say.** TR: 64

3 **Cut out the cards on page 61.** Glue the cards. Say.

☺ I like...   ☹ I don't like...

4 **What is your favorite food?** Draw.

28

5 **Listen and color.** Listen, count, and say. TR: 65

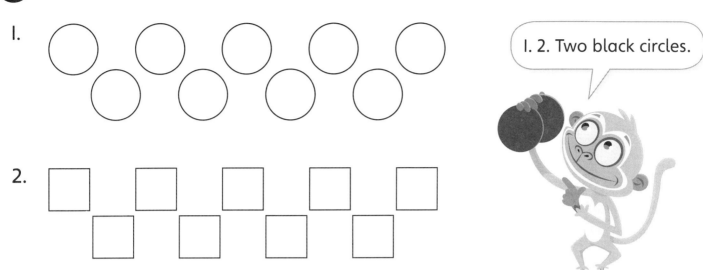

1. 2. Two black circles.

6 **Count and say.** How many circles? How many squares?

circles ___

squares ___

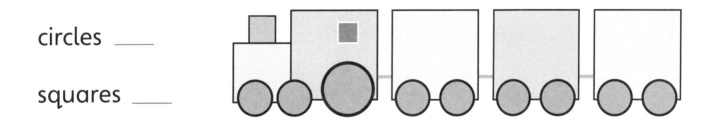

7 **Listen.** Count and say. TR: 66

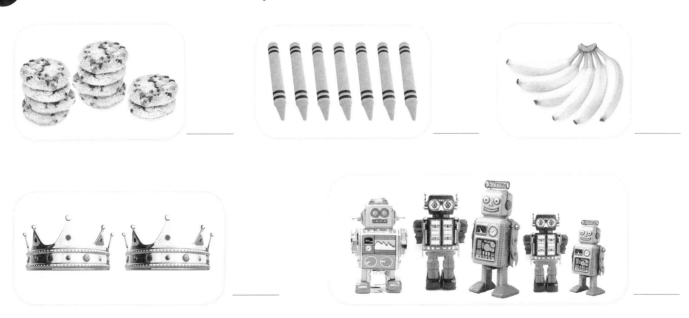

29

8 Listen and say. TR: 67

9 Listen and look. Which word is different? Circle. TR: 68

10 Listen and chant. Say a new verse. TR: 69

Unit 7
Clothes

1 **Listen and look.** Draw a line. TR: 70

2 **Listen and look.** Draw a line. Color. TR: 71

3 **Listen and say.** TR: 72

It's hot. I'm wearing shorts.

It's cold. He's wearing a hat.

4 **Cut out the cards on page 63.** Listen. Glue the cards. Say. TR: 73

5 **Connect the dots.** What is it? Say. Color.

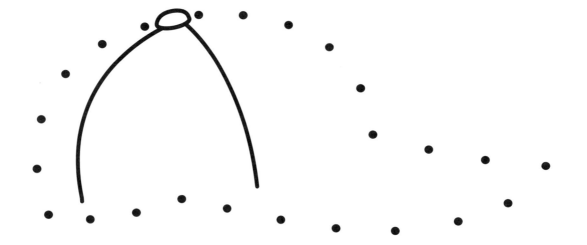

6 **Listen.** Color and say. TR: 74

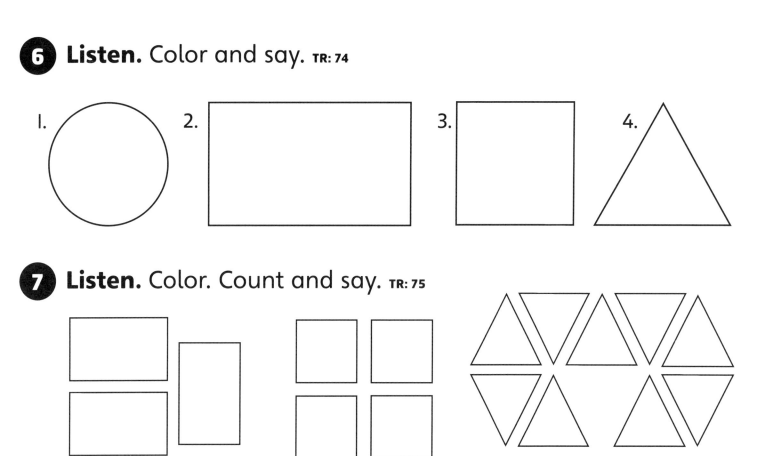

7 **Listen.** Color. Count and say. TR: 75

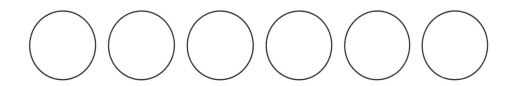

8 **Listen.** Count and write. TR: 76

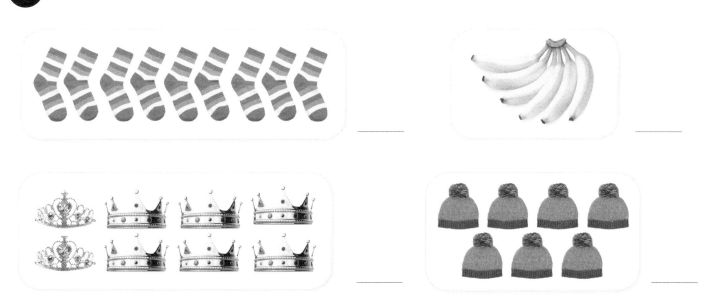

33

9 **Listen and say.** TR: 77

10 **Listen and look.** Which word is different? Circle. TR: 78

1.

2.

3.

11 **Listen and chant.** Say a new verse. TR: 79

I want a

My sister wants a

Let's shop for clothes.

 please say yes!

I want some

My sister wants a

We want new clothes.

 please say yes!

34

Unit 8
Animals

1 **Listen and look.** Draw a line. TR: 80

2 Listen and say. TR: 81

3 Cut out the cards on page 63. Listen. Glue the cards. Say. TR: 82

4 Connect the dots. What is it? Say. Color.

5 **Listen.** Color and say. TR: 83

6 **Listen.** Color. Count and say. TR: 84

7 **Listen.** Count and write. TR: 85

8 **Listen and say.** TR: 86

9 **Listen and look.** Which word is different? Circle. TR: 87

1.

2.

3.

10 **Listen and chant.** Say a new verse. TR: 88

Look, I'm a
I walk and I run.

Look, I'm a
I walk and I run.

Look, I'm a
standing in the sun.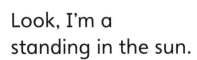

Look, I'm a
standing in the sun.

38

Units 5-8
Review

1 **Listen.** Look and circle. TR: 89

2 Listen. Look and circle. TR: 90

1.

2.

3.

3 Listen and color. TR: 91

4 Listen. Count and circle. TR: 92

1.     2.

3.    4.

5.   6.

Unit 1   Use with Activity 3 on page 6.

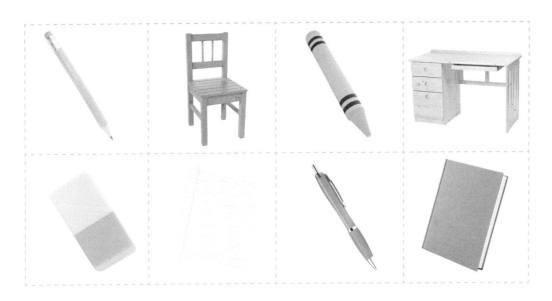

Unit 2   Use with Activity 3 on page 10.

57

Unit 3   Use with Activity 5 on page 14.

Unit 4   Use with Activity 4 on page 18.

Unit 5 Use with Activity 4 on page 24.

Unit 6 Use with Activity 3 on page 28.

Unit 7 Use with Activity 4 on page 32.

Unit 8 Use with Activity 3 on page 36.

63